SERVING PATRONS WITH DISABILITIES

SERVING PATRONS with DISABILITIES

Perspectives and Insights from People with Disabilities

EDITED BY KODI LASKIN

CHICAGO | 2023

KODI LASKIN, a graduate of Rollins College, has used her unique position as both a library assistant and a service animal handler to develop a training geared for libraries and businesses to learn about laws regarding service animals and their place in society that is available through SEFLIN and NEFLIN. She and her service animal, Piper, can still be found frequenting any and all libraries they come across.

ISBNs
978-0-8389-3731-0 (paper)
978-0-8389-3955-0 (PDF)
978-0-8389-3863-8 (ePub)

Library of Congress Cataloging-in-Publication Data

Names: Laskin, Kodi, editor.
Title: Serving patrons with disabilities : perspectives and insights from people with disabilities / edited by Kodi Laskin.
Description: Chicago : ALA Editions, 2023. | Includes bibliographical references and index. | Summary: "This book provides library workers with the tools they need to provide excellent customer service and a safe environment to all patrons regardless of ability"—Provided by publisher.
Identifiers: LCCN 2022049943 (print) | LCCN 2022049944 (ebook) | ISBN 9780838937310 (paperback) | ISBN 9780838939550 (pdf) | ISBN 9780838938638 (epub)
Subjects: LCSH: Libraries and people with disabilities—United States.
Classification: LCC Z711.92.H3 S47 2023 (print) | LCC Z711.92.H3 (ebook) | DDC 027.6/63—dc23/eng/20221031
LC record available at https://lccn.loc.gov/2022049943
LC ebook record available at https://lccn.loc.gov/2022049944

Book design by Alejandra Diaz in the Proforma and Korolev typefaces.

♾ This paper meets the requirements of ANSI/NISO Z39.48-1992 (Permanence of Paper).

Printed in the United States of America
27 26 25 24 23 5 4 3 2 1

CONTENTS

INTRODUCTION
Disability Is Not a Bad Word

Kodi Laskin

We, as a society, have a problem talking about disability. Part of this issue has to do with lack of understanding, and part of it has to do with people's discomfort talking about the subject. But what if there was an easier way? What if there was a way to bridge the gap between people with disabilities and those without so that no one feels like they don't have the information they need to interact with patrons regardless of ability?

The purpose of this book is to give those who work in libraries the tools they need to provide excellent customer service and a safe environment for all patrons regardless of ability. Accessibility has been a hot topic issue of late, including the final ruling on Section 508 of the Rehabilitation Act of 1973 regarding website accessibility and the emergence of service animals and the abuse of service animal law. The best way to be sure that everyone is not only upholding the law, but also making their library open and accessible to all is to be well informed.

This book is written by people with disabilities, and the stories within give a brief look into what it's like to be in the shoes of someone with a disability. The goal is not only to encourage a more empathetic staff, but also to open the lines of communication and provide better understanding for why a patron might have an odd request, or why compassion and understanding are paramount. This book will show, through real examples, why these extra steps are important.

An important thing to keep in mind when interacting with patrons is person-first vs. identity-first language. When speaking to a person, they might prefer being referred to as a person with a disability or as a disabled person. Person-first language is meant to show that even though the person might have a difference from the norm, they are a person first. Identity-first language, in contrast, is used as a way to show that the disability is nothing to be ashamed of and can instead be an empowering fact. In general, this is a personal choice for the person, but there are some groups who tend to prefer one or the other. If you aren't sure, the best practice is to ask. Most people would rather answer a question you might find awkward then be identified in a way that makes them uncomfortable. We all want to make sure our patrons feel comfortable not only being in the library, but also asking us for assistance when needed.

Americans with Disabilities Act: At a Glance

Throughout this book, we'll refer to the Americans with Disabilities Act (ADA). Here's some brief information that covers the basics of what ADA is. The ADA

- was ratified in 1990 with an amendment in 2008 that changed the definition of *disability*,
- is a civil rights law that prohibits discrimination against people with disabilities in all areas of public life, and
- is divided into five sections, each of which focuses on a different area of public life.

For more information, please visit www.ada.gov.

CHAPTER ONE

SERVICE ANIMALS

Kodi Laskin

I walk into the restaurant with my fiancé and my service dog, Piper. It's our first time at this place, so I feel a spike of nervousness. The room is relatively small with tables crowded in, barely enough room to walk single file down the row. The hostess bustles through; she's an expert at avoiding all the waiters milling about. I see her eyes fall on Piper and my heart stops. What's going to happen next? Will she ask us to leave? Will I have to explain the law? I don't want to have to do this.

Her eyes flick between Piper and I for a second before her hostess smile graces her face and she asks, "Table for two?" We nod and follow her as she leads us past five, six, seven empty four-top tables to a small, two-top table in the back corner completely isolated from any other patrons. Of course, Piper can fit anywhere without issue, but I usually prefer the bigger table to let her stretch out. My fiancé settles in, but I don't feel right. I can't prove it, but it feels like we were put here deliberately, and the thought of that puts me on edge.

Piper settles in at my feet under the table, her head resting on the top of my shoe. It takes a second for the waiter to notice us, but the experience after that is relatively pleasant. Piper falls asleep before our entrees are delivered, her tongue sticking out on my ankle. The patrons who were seated when we arrived have since left, and none of the tables around us have been filled.

After our check is returned, we stand, and Piper emerges from the table to stand next to me. The waiter stops, staring at her. "Oh, wow. I didn't even know she was there. Are you training her?"

"Oh no," I reply, "I'm not that good. She was trained by a professional."

"Oh . . . so she's for you?" he asks.

"Yep," I nod, feeling uncomfortable.

"She must be the real deal; it's like she wasn't there at all."

"She was very well trained," my fiancé cuts in. "Just doing her job."

With another smile we both head out, snaking our way through the tables, ignoring the comments of people who hadn't seen us walk in. It's a relief to be back in the car; Piper settled into the back seat, on our way home. ☙

What You Need to Know about Service Animals

If you google the words "service animals" you'll find hundreds of links ranging from copies of the Americans with Disabilities Act (ADA) to websites offering a full package of materials to make your dog a legitimate service animal. Even in the profession of information literacy it can be difficult to discern fact from fiction. This section will break down everything you need to know about service animals, including how they're trained, what they're trained to do, and the logistics surrounding the laws covering service animals and their handlers.

The ADA

The ADA, enacted in 1990 to preserve the rights of people with disabilities, has a section on service animals. In this section, service animals are defined as "dogs that are individually trained to do work or perform tasks for people with disabilities."[1] Broken down, this law means that for this dog to be considered a service animal, the handler must have a disability, and the dog must be trained to do something to help the handler who has a disability. This is why, while working, a service animal is considered a medical device. There is no list of accepted or rejected disabilities. Because there's no doctor involvement, it's at the discretion of the handler to decide if their disability could benefit from the use of a service animal. The handler, usually in partnership with either a trainer or a nonprofit organization, determines if their condition would benefit by having a trained dog. There is a tradeoff that must be considered as well. As much as I hope this book and my trainings help, there's a lot of attention that comes with having a service animal, not all of which is kind or wanted. I no longer have the opportunity to go places unnoticed. People with service animals aren't able to blend into the background. It also adds a layer of difficulty preparing to go anywhere. Much like leaving the house with a child, a handler must pack for themselves and for their dog.

These animals are not required to wear a vest, have an ID tag, or have any identifying badges or features to prove that the dog is a working animal. In general, I have my dog in a vest while she's working because it's easier for other patrons to identify her, but there are simple reasons why a vest can be an inaccessible requirement. There are people who, due to any number of impairments, might not have the fine motor skills required to put a vest on a dog. Another example is dogs used for autism support; while performing deep pressure therapy, the buckle of a belt could be uncomfortable on the handler. The ADA allows two questions if the dog can't be immediately identified as a service animal: (1) Is the dog a service animal required because of a disability? and (2) What work or task has the dog been trained to perform?[2] Essentially these two questions are there to make sure the two conditions are met.

As a library employee, these questions can be awkward and uncomfortable, but they are essential; it's the only tool provided to ensure the animal is a service animal. Of course, someone could lie, but according to the law, the two questions are what we have to use. On the other hand, as a service animal handler, I love answering questions. When library staff approach me and ask them, I feel more at ease knowing that I won't have to fight for the right to have my medical device with me. They know the law, I answer the questions happily, and go about my day.

Training

A service animal must be trained, either by handlers themselves if they feel capable, a nonprofit organization, or a professional trainer. Their training can take anywhere from one to three years and cost up to $40,000 depending on what service the animal is being trained to provide. None of these costs are covered by insurance and oftentimes the waiting list for a dog provided free of charge from a nonprofit organization can be one to three years.

Training can start as early as six months with basic commands and socialization. It's important that these dogs are exposed to as many types of people and places as possible, so they'll learn they're safe in all situations. Public access training is determined by the dog but will start at dog friendly locations like parks and pet supply stores before moving into other areas like grocery stores and libraries. Up until this point, which can take anywhere from three to nine months, the animal can't be considered a service animal; it's just a very well-trained dog. It's not until the dog is task trained, learning the specific task or tasks it will do to alleviate the person's disability that the animal shifts to service animal status.

The choice that a service animal would be beneficial isn't taken lightly by those in the disabled community because of the time and financial burden incurred. From experience, the benefit of having Piper with me, and knowing that I'm safe even if something unexpected happens, has been well worth the cost.

Tasks

When you ask a handler what service their animal provides, it's important to know that there can be a variety of answers. Service animals can learn more than 100 commands ranging from "sit" to "grab my meds." The types of tasks can be grouped into five major categories each with tasks and training that is more specific to the handler's disability. The five categories include: medical alert, mobility assist, autism support, seeing eye, and psychiatric. When a handler answers the second question, a response of "medical alert" is just as acceptable as a more specific answer like "seizure alert." These simple statements cover a vast array of specific tasks that can be life changing to a disabled patron.

A note to remember: when a patron walks into the library and states that their dog is a mobility assist animal, we can't disagree because we don't see a wheelchair or a cane. The animal might pick up dropped items or function as a stability device. Not all disabilities are visible, and when we ask the two questions, it's not to determine what the person's disability is. We ask to verify that the animal has been trained to perform a task to help with a disability.

The only unacceptable answers to what task an animal is trained to perform include emotional support, therapy, and assistance. The last example is too vague and doesn't describe an actual task. We'll discuss emotional support and therapy in a later section.

Breeds

It's never our place as employees to determine if a dog is suitable for the job it's been trained to perform. While most nonprofit organizations will use golden retrievers or Labradors for their temperament and ease of training, there is no list of acceptable and unacceptable breeds for service work. The only limitations are what jobs a dog can and cannot do. For example, it would be almost impossible for a Chihuahua to work as a mobility assistance dog. In fact, that type of work requires clearance from a vet due to the pressure being put on the animal's joints. The breeds you'd be more likely to see in your library working as mobility assistance dogs would be retrievers or German Shepherds. Other popular breeds include poodles and poodle mixes due to their hypoallergenic fur.

I'm often asked if small dogs can be real service dogs, and the short answer is yes. Some people have noticed that Papillons are unusually good at detecting seizures. It can be convenient to have a smaller dog work as a diabetic alert dog because they can be carried in a pouch, keeping them close to the handler's mouth, where the scent of high and low blood sugar can be detected, though large dogs can be used for this task as well.

It's important to note that a breed cannot be discriminated against if it's a trained service animal. Even if there's a countywide restriction or a restriction at an apartment complex, a person cannot be denied access for having their animal with them. The only reason to deny access due to the kind of breed is if the animal is too large to fit into the space, therefore hindering the activity of the business or store, for example. Libraries generally don't face these issues. As a handler with a service dog who looks like a pit bull from the front, I have had interesting reactions from people when Piper and I are out in public—from people screaming and running away to people asking me if I really think a pit bull is a safe choice for the public in general. A dog's temperament isn't breed specific regardless of the stigmas that exist.

A quick note about service animals that I think is wonderful and interesting. Miniature horses can also be service animals. They must be housebroken, under the control of the handler, and like their dog counterparts, perform a task to assist a person with a disability. Miniature pony service animals have been known to be seeing eye and mobility assist animals. They can be preferable to dogs due to their longer life span and larger build. They are very rare, and in my time working, I've never seen one, but they do exist and are legally covered by the ADA.

Handlers and Trainers

There's a misconception that service animals are only used for those with sight impairments, so anyone who can obviously see or doesn't seem to fit into that category must be a trainer instead. Service animals can be used for a wide array of tasks, from cardiac arrest or diabetic alerts to mobility assist to Post-Traumatic Stress Disorder assistance. The assumption that service animals are only used by the sight-impaired population demonstrates a lack of education and knowledge by the general public. This can be a red flag for handlers and could possibly lead them to hesitate making return trips to your library. When faced with a handler and service animal in your library, assume the person is a handler unless you're told otherwise. While people don't normally offer up this information readily, they might when asked the two questions. Whether or not a service animal in training is given the right of public access is outlined in state law and is therefore not covered in the ADA. For example, in my state, Florida statute 413.08 section 8 gives trainers who are actively training an animal for service the same public access afforded to a fully trained service animal with their disabled handler. So, when asked the two questions, an answer of, "I'm training the animal" could be an acceptable answer depending on the state. In general, a trainer will know when an animal is ready to be out in public and will be equipped to manage any challenges the animal might face in unknown circumstances. A trainer wouldn't knowingly bring a dog into an unsafe situation, but public places can be unpredictable. Trainers are well equipped to handle the dog's anxieties and uncertainties in a new situation. It's always a good idea to keep an eye out to make sure a service animal and handler are okay in the same way we keep an eye on all our patrons to make sure they're okay. In my experience, I don't think it's necessary to watch service animals in training any closer than their fully trained counterparts.

Emotional Support Animals

With the questions come responses such as "emotional support" and "therapy." As neither of these are considered tasks covered by the ADA, neither should be given the right of public access. To have a proper emotional support animal, the person must have a note from a doctor stating need. These animals are not service animals. Not only are they not limited by the ADA because they're not covered by it—meaning they can be any animal (including peacocks)—they also aren't required to have any training. None. The only places that aren't pet friendly, where emotional support animals are legally allowed, are the cabin of an aircraft and in a residence regardless of policy and without fees. The ADA specifically states, "These terms are used to describe animals that provide comfort just by being with a person. Because they have not been trained to perform a specific job or task, they do not qualify as service animals under the ADA."[3] In general, the hope is that a person with an animal trained to perform a task to mitigate a disability wouldn't say emotional support as an answer to the second question because that disqualifies the animal from public access.

What to Do with Service Animals in Your Library

It's easy to read about law and accessibility; it's another thing to actually put it into practice. This section will break down the steps to take when a service animal team walks into your library.

Know the Guidelines

Read the questions out loud until they feel comfortable to ask. Is this dog a service animal required because of a disability? What work or task have they been trained to perform? That can be a mouthful. I've found it helpful to print out the two questions and tape them to the staff computers; having them easily accessible can help in the moment. It can also be helpful to have copies of the ADA guidelines on service animals at the desk in case a patron has a question or is uncertain of why you're asking them what service the animal provides. In my experience, people will have no problem saying "yes" to the first question but might push back on the second, believing you're asking them the specifics of their disability. In this circumstance, it's easier to explain that these are the questions allowed by the ADA with a copy of the document readily available if you need it.

The unfortunate truth about having a service animal is that you give up a certain level of privacy. My disability is no longer invisible while I'm with Piper because her presence alone confirms that I have a disability; if I didn't have one, she wouldn't be with me. The second question only asks what the dog does. So, for example, I could say that Piper is a seizure alert service animal, or, if I want to be more vague, I could say she's trained as a medical alert service animal. The task she performs is alerting me to an impending medical occurrence. Some patrons might be upset at the perceived invasion into their privacy. But, to assure that the two qualifications that define a service animal are met, both questions must be answered satisfactorily. If they aren't, we can't identify the animal as a service animal and as such, need to ask the person to remove the animal from the library.

Ask the Right Questions

As a service animal handler, I understand the inclination to look at her and smile and to want to pet her. My hope is that after that initial reaction of seeing a dog, the next choice is to not comment on it. One of the hardest things about being a handler is being treated like Piper's mouthpiece, constantly telling people about her breed and age and how her day is going. When you come across a service animal team in your library, it will be tempting to ask about their dog. Resist. Ask them if they need help finding a book or would like information on your programing. By acting as though the dog isn't there and engaging the handler with questions common to the library, you can make them feel welcome and they'll likely feel comfortable returning. The only thing that should be different in your interaction with the handler and any other patron is asking the two questions first. After that, they're just another person coming to take advantage of the resources of the library.

Spot Out-of-Control Behavior

While we do need to accept an appropriate answer, we also need to watch for out-of-control behavior from the animal. This clause within the ADA is vague on purpose. It's imperative to remember that at the end of the day, they're dogs, not robots; sometimes they'll make mistakes. Every once in a while, Piper will be startled and bark, just once, and will almost always lay down afterwards and look up at me. This isn't out-of-control behavior. I've also been known to exclaim when I'm startled. I can't blame her for doing the same thing. If, however, she started barking and didn't stop no matter how many times I told her to, that would be out-of-control behavior. Other examples include jumping on people or furniture, lunging at people, or any disturbing action that can't be stopped by the handler. If the dog displays any of these behaviors, it is appropriate to ask the handler to remove the animal. If the dog has been identified as a service animal based on the answers to the two questions but displays out-of-control behavior leading to its removal, the handler must be given the same goods or services they would have received, but without the animal present. One way to accommodate this in a library setting would be to ask the person what books they were looking for and bring the items to them outside.

Much like when asking the two questions, I would recommend bringing a copy of the ADA guidelines with you when confronting a patron with an out-of-control animal. It's important to state that you are asking them to remove the animal due to the behavior of the dog, but that you would be happy to help in any way possible without the animal present. It's never acceptable to offer to hold the animal as that puts the responsibility of safety for the animal and those in the immediate vicinity on you. It's also important to insist that the person remove the dog, even if they just want to do one quick thing. By maintaining a standard, you're showing that the library is a safe place for everyone, and inappropriate behavior won't be accepted regardless of species.

Dealing with Pushback

Personally, I don't like confrontation. If there's a more pleasant way to go about a situation, I'll try that type of option. But when it comes to safety, there needs to be a bottom line. If your library is not pet friendly, the bottom line is that only service animals specifically trained to help a person with a disability that are house trained and under the control of the handler can be allowed inside. I've compiled a list of pushbacks that I have received, and the solutions we've come up with to handle them.

Here's My Dog's ID Card

According to the ADA, there is no federally mandated ID card for service animals. There are a number of websites you can visit. For a fee, you can send in a picture of your dog that will be put on a card and mailed to you. This in no way verifies the animal's legitimacy either way. There are some handlers who carry IDs for convenience. I'm personally against the practice as it propagates the belief that an ID is an acceptable form of proof that the animal is a service animal.

Example of What to Say

"Thank you for showing me the ID, but I require answers to the questions to verify that this is a service animal."

You Can't Ask Me What My Disability Is

When we ask the second question, we aren't asking what their disability is, though it can be misinterpreted that way. It is, of course, our hope that if someone is utilizing the right to use an assistance animal, they will know the laws that allow them to do so; not knowing the laws doesn't negate legitimacy. This is an example of a good time to have the ADA laws handy to show the patron.

Example of What to Say

"I assure you I would never ask that. Here's a copy of the ADA laws on service animals. I'm asking the two questions defined here to identify your animal as a service animal."

I Have a Doctor's Note

A doctor's note is only required for an emotional support animal, which is not given the right of public access. Furthermore, though a doctor can assess the need for an assistance animal, they wouldn't be able to quantify the training the animal has received. Therefore, a doctor's note is not sufficient evidence that an animal is a service animal.

Example of What to Say

"I don't need to see the note; instead, could you answer these two questions for me?"

I'll Only Be a Minute

While it would be simple to just let the patron finish their business, there are two big issues with this approach: (1) That the ADA as it's written isn't important enough for you to enforce it; and (2) that the safety of the other patrons in the library isn't as important as this patron having their animal with them. This confrontation is difficult but ultimately worth it, as chances are the patron won't try the same tactic again. By doing so, you're part of a bigger movement to stop people from abusing this law.

Example of What to Say

"I understand that you have a quick task; however, we do have a policy that pets aren't allowed in the library. I would be happy to assist you when you return without the dog."

My Dog Has Its Vest

Wearing a vest doesn't make an animal a service animal. The internet is flooded with sellers who could provide a vest made of almost any material with any number of patches on it. This doesn't even count the fact that a vest isn't necessary on a trained service animal. While most handlers will work their dog in a vest for ease of explaining to the public, it doesn't serve as proof.

Example of What to Say

"Of course, and I'm sure you've heard these questions before. I would appreciate it if you would answer them again for me."

It's Okay, My Dog Goes with Me Everywhere/ I Can't Leave My Dog at Home Alone

This is part of the problem. To avoid conflict, staff at libraries, stores, and restaurants will see someone with a dog and just say nothing. The more places that allow people to exploit this oversight, the more entitled they become. But when it comes down to it, there's a library policy for a reason and that policy generally only allows service animals in the building.

Example of What to Say

"I understand that; however, we do have a policy against pets in the library. I would be happy to assist you at another time without the dog present."

I've Brought My Dog in Here Hundreds of Times Before

True or not, this statement doesn't negate the fact that the person should respond to the two questions to any person who asks them.

Example of What to Say

"I'm glad you've come to visit us again! Unfortunately, I haven't seen you yet. Would you mind answering the questions for me?"

Service Animal Approaches: At a Glance

- **Know the guidelines:** Read the questions aloud until they feel natural to say.
- **Ask the right questions:** Avoid asking prying questions about the dog; keep it about the person.
- **Spot out-of-control behavior:** Mistakes happen, but consistent disruptive behavior is out of control.
- **Dealing with pushback:** Safety is more important than avoiding conflict.

Next Steps

The easiest way to solve the misunderstandings about service animals is education. An easy step to take is to have a printout of the ADA laws on service animals at all desks in case there's a problem with a patron. Another simple idea is to have the two questions readily available at every desk for staff. When it comes down to it, though, training is imperative. If every staff member knew the two questions and had a working understanding of the law and why it's important, it would not only make the life of handlers such as myself easier, but it would also promote a safer environment for all.

One part of training that is, in my opinion, more important than memorizing the questions, is knowing what is and isn't an acceptable answer. It's easiest to remember the categories: mobility assist, medical alert and response, seeing eye, autism support, and psychiatric. It's important to remember that not all disabilities are visible, and it's not our place to decide if someone is legally disabled.

I know from my own experience as a public library staff member that the confrontation around asking and receiving answers to these questions can be stressful. I feel my heart race and my hands shake every time I encounter a library customer accompanied by an animal because I'm not sure how they'll react. Will the person yell that I can't ask them that? Will the person shove an ID card they bought online in my face? Will they answer with a practiced calm answer? I'm never sure. So, I do understand the thought of, "Well, this is probably fine. The dog is small. The dog is in a stroller. The person will probably be in and out quick." We've already discussed how this issue can lead to the misconception that it's okay to bring in a dog because no one will stop them. What we haven't discussed are the safety issues.

The Chihuahua in the stroller doesn't seem like a threat, but I've experienced one jumping out of the stroller to attack my working dog. I've had dogs on retractable leashes run around the desk to see Piper, and others that wouldn't stop barking after seeing her. In each of these situations, my life as a handler is at risk. If my dog is attacked, lunged at, or barked at, she may miss an alert. If she's hurt, I'm in danger until she's okay to work again. I personally know how hard it is to ask someone to remove the dog; we never want to turn someone away from the library. But when you really look at the situation the person with the Emotional Support Animal (ESA), or even just a pet, can return without the animal because they don't need the animal to function. I can't just go somewhere without Piper. I need her to make sure that I'm able to safely function as well as anyone else. That ESA makes it unsafe for me to be in the library, and I don't have a choice about bringing her with me. Instead of thinking of it as excluding someone, rephrase: "We would be happy to assist you without the animal present. We aren't excluding someone, we're making sure it's safe for everyone, including the patron who needs a service animal."

A problem I've often come across on both ends is the insistence of an ID. As a handler, I wish there was a federally mandated identification card that requires handler application, provides proof, and is accepted at all public locations. It would make my life easier to only need to show a card. However, as is, this isn't a federal system. In fact, the ADA specifically states that an ID isn't necessary to prove the animal is a service animal. It's quite simple to go online, search for service animal, and click on any number of websites that will ask you to check two boxes, pay anywhere from $50-$100 and a card will be sent to you saying your animal is a service animal regardless of training or need. The biggest problem I've run across with this is that people will buy these—I admit they look legitimate—and show them to local restaurants and stores. So, when I visit the restaurant or store and don't have an ID card, they'll think I'm the one trying to bring an untrained dog into public. There have been countless times I've been asked to leave because I didn't have a card, even after showing the staff a copy of the ADA. There are some legitimate service animal teams who use an ID card because it's easy. I don't agree with this line of thought because I don't believe we should continue the false belief that ID cards are a valid way of identifying service animals. Regardless of whether or not the patron shows an ID, the two questions must be asked and answered to officially identify a service animal.

The only other reason to ask a person to remove their service animal is if the animal isn't housebroken. In defense of handlers who may have had an animal have an accident in a public place, sometimes dogs don't feel well and don't have a way to communicate that, or maybe the handler was in a rush and just didn't notice. Dogs can get startled and have accidents. It is, of course, the responsibility of the handler to clean up after their dog, and it is appropriate to ask them to leave, though chances are they'll notice that their dog isn't feeling well and will leave on their own. While I recognize that this can be frustrating for an animal to have an accident in the library—especially an animal that is supposed to be highly trained—do keep in mind that they're not robots, and it might have legitimately been an accident. It would be appropriate to follow the patron and the animal out, but it isn't a lifelong ban. If the patron were to return the next day the only thing to be done is to ask the two questions again and ask if they need help finding anything, as you would with any other patron. If the problem is persistent, I would speak to someone higher up about what steps to take. Accidents happen, but the ADA does clearly state that the animal must be housebroken.

This need for education goes beyond just staff. With all the misinformation about service animals circulating, patrons may be confused on what their rights are either in seeking a service animal, or in being around a service animal, and often don't know where to look for accurate information. Making sure the ADA guidelines are easily accessible can help to alleviate these problems. Having well-informed staff can lead to well-informed patrons. Patrons soon realize that staff have what could be an out-of-control situation in hand, and that assurance can avoid future problems.

Story Redo

This time, instead of walking into a restaurant, I walk into your library. It's our first time visiting, so I feel my usual jitters. The librarian at the reference desk notices Piper and my heart stops. Will I be asked to leave?

> The woman approaches me with a smile, papers in hand. "Hello," she says, looking directly at me, "I'm sure you've been asked these before, but is your animal a service animal required because of a disability?"
>
> I exhale the breath I didn't even know I was holding. "Yes, she is."
>
> "Thank you. And what work or task is she trained to perform?"
>
> I can feel the weight lift off my shoulders. It's safe. "She's a medical alert dog."
>
> "Thank you for answering. Is there anything I can help you with?"
>
> "Yes, actually. I saw a class online I was interested in."
>
> "The writing class? I'll actually be teaching that. I'll be in this room to the right. I don't think anyone is in there, so you'll have your choice of seats. I think we have about 10 minutes or so before we'll start."
>
> I smile. "Brilliant. I'll look around a bit."
>
> With a smile the woman nods and returns to the desk. I head off into the stacks, eyes on the titles of books for the one that will stand out. We pass through with no issue. One patron notices us, but we're able to go into the room where I settle Piper beneath my chair. We go through the class with no issue, and I plan to return to the next session in two weeks. I leave and go to the front desk to apply for my library card, safe in the knowledge that while in the building I'll be safe and sure I won't be harassed. ☙

NOTES

1. ADA: Americans With Disabilities Act of 1990, Pub. L. No. 101–336, § 35.136, 104 Stat. 328 (1990; amended 2010).
2. ADA, § 35.136.
3. U.S. Department of Justice, "Frequently Asked Questions about Service Animals and the ADA," ADA, July 20, 2015, https://www.ada.gov/regs2010/service_animal_qa.html.

CHAPTER TWO

MOBILITY AIDS

Leah Keevan

She approaches the door and attempts to open it. It's heavy and almost doesn't budge. She throws her effort into it and wedges it open, pulling herself halfway in but she's stopped abruptly by the seemingly insurmountable sill of the door frame. With effort she grips the edges of the door and yanks herself through, the wheels of her walker bouncing over the sill and onto the decorative carpet inside. The wheels feel like they're slogging through mud until she makes it to the uneven tile. She feels every bump but at least she's able to move.

It takes a moment to find a catalog computer at her height; all she sees in the front are at standing level. The book she needs is on a higher shelf. She musters all her strength to stand and grab it, and she feels embarrassed when she notices someone staring. She sits back down and resets herself before wheeling back to the front, passing the self-checkout stations that are at standing height to the counter that thankfully does have a lower checkout station. ☙

Mobility Aids: What You Need to Know

Have you ever used or taken care of someone with a mobility aid? If you haven't, you might not be aware just how difficult aids can make traversing the world. There are many different reasons to need a mobility aid, and many different types in a variety of styles but each have their own issues in day-to-day life. The most common mobility aids are canes, crutches, walkers, and wheelchairs. Canes, crutches, and walkers are all used to make walking easier and safer for their users, while wheelchairs are used by those who cannot walk safely. Mobility aids are used by people of all ages, and at times, the reason the aid is needed is not easily recognized.

A common misconception with mobility aids is that the user is completely reliant upon it 100 percent of the time. While there are instances where a person is unable to negotiate daily life without the assistance of a device, many people are partially dependent and either use mobility aids in times of great need, or as an extra security measure to ensure their safety while out in public. Regardless, it's never the place of others to determine what a person is capable of or to determine a patron's mobility needs. Thankfully, there are actions you can take to make things more accessible, safer, and easier for everyone. The ADA is a legal document that both prohibits discrimination against those with disabilities and details specifications on how public buildings should be laid out to be accessible for all.

The most important thing to keep in mind when striving for an accessible library is space. While that hallway might be simple for a person to walk through, it might be impossible to navigate for a person with the extra width of a wheelchair, or it may be too long for someone using a walker. One goal of the library is to house and display as many books as possible, but if a patron isn't able to navigate the shelves, it'll all be for naught.

Improving Outdoor Accessibility

The best place to start the process towards accessibility is before you even enter the building. One important aspect for being accessible is parking. The ADA requires library parking lots to have at least one accessible parking spot for every 25 parking places. These parking spots

- must be eight feet by eight feet with a white-striped aisle for wheelchair vans,
- should be marked with a sign, and
- be as close to the accessible door as possible.

Keeping the area around and between accessible parking spaces clear is a must as the striped area can make the difference between a patron being able to put down a ramp or otherwise enter their vehicle.

The path towards the main accessible entrance should be at least 36 inches wide and made of a hard, smooth material with no barriers. If the building has steps, it must also have ramps with handrails that are between 34–38 inches tall. The ramp must have a 1:12 slope, meaning for every inch of height for the ramp, there must be 12 inches of length to the ramp. If the ramp is longer than 30 feet, there must be a rest platform. While it might seem tedious to think about such a small thing as the slope of the ramp, I'd encourage you to pay attention the next time you walk up an incline. Your body needs to work a little harder to get to where you're going. Requiring a mobility device adds another layer of complication to this process as you're not just moving your own body up the incline; you're also using either something to help maintain balance, doesn't require all your limbs, or has wheels, all of which make inclines difficult at best. By requiring a certain slope, the ADA is making the situation at least a little easier.

There should be no barriers for book returns; they should be easily accessible by wheelchair and ideally, they should be placed next to the accessible path into the library. Barriers can mean anything from decorative signs to trees. They should also be accessible via a paved path without the need to travel on grass or dirt. The doorway should be at least 36 inches wide, and the threshold must be no taller than ¼ inch tall and should be easy to open with one hand for those with mobility aids. If possible, an automatic door with a button for a wheelchair user to open the door is ideal. If not possible, a light door with a handle you don't need to turn is the next best option. If there's an inaccessible entrance as well, there should be a sign directing patrons towards the accessible entrance to make it easier to find.

Improving Indoor Accessibility

Inside the library, the floors should be flat and smooth. If there are ramps in the library, there should be a strip of color at the beginning of them to warn people that the floor isn't flat. This might seem like an arbitrary request but knowing that the floor won't be flat changes how a person walks and the paths taken. While patrons who are not living with disabilities might be able to make that adjustment as it's happening, patrons with mobility aids will need the warning to be able to prepare how they will navigate a good and safe path for themselves. Pathways should be at least 32 inches wide to allow wheelchairs to pass through unimpeded, and places where two wheelchairs might have to pass each other should be at least 60 inches wide. If there are any end caps, the width of the aisles should be measured between end caps and not the original shelves.

If there are multiple stories to the library, there should be an accessible elevator and signs directing patrons towards it. If there are stairs, they should be at least 36 inches wide, and each step should be no more than 11 inches tall. The stairs should all be non-slip and have handrails.

There are many issues that can arise in the stacks of the library. Ideally no shelves should be higher than 48 inches, but if they are, put a sign saying that assistance to reach things on higher shelves is available from a library staff member. Most people consider higher shelves inaccessible to those with mobility aids, but they don't consider the fact that lower shelves are just as bad. It's difficult enough for someone in a wheelchair to bend down to the ground level, but it's dangerous for someone using a cane or walker as they can lose stability. Having easily accessible chairs that people with aids can sit on to look over lower shelves would be beneficial. It would also be helpful to have baskets or bags for people to hold their books in while browsing so they only need one hand to hold them. This keeps their other hand free to hold onto their mobility aid. The checkout counter and help desk should be no taller than 36 inches so it's reachable by those in a wheelchair. If it's not possible to make the entire desk low, making a section of the counter lower to accommodate wheelchair users is a great solution.

When placing signs, please consider those in wheelchairs and place them lower, about chest level of a standing adult, so they can be seen by all or large enough to see from any height. All bathrooms should be labeled as accessible or not accessible, and the pathway towards the elevator and exit should be clearly marked.

If there are computer stations, they should have at least 36 inches of clear space around them. At least three of the computers should be at a level easily accessible for wheelchairs. The desktops should be between 28–38 inches from the floor with a clearance of at least 27 inches beneath the desk for the legs of those in wheelchairs to be able to fit. The depth of the desk from the edge of the desk to the wall it is against must be between 17–25 inches. There should be a minimum width of

30 inches from one end of the workspace to the next for the knees of a seated individual to fit. If there are more than three computers at the library, some computer spaces don't have to be accessible. Should there be furniture in the library, there should be at least 40 inches of clear space between the pieces of furniture. All tables should have a clearance of at least 27 inches high and a depth of 17–25 inches for wheelchair users to be able to use the tables.

Bathroom accessibility is so important and unfortunately often overlooked. One of the most important aspects for accessibility is clear space. In an accessible restroom stall, the sink shouldn't be mounted above 34 inches with ample space around the sink (the door can't swing into the space around the sink for the area to be considered compliant), and space beneath the sink for the legs of wheelchair users. The toilet seat height should be 17–19 inches with grab rails mounted along the walls. There should be a clear circle of 60 inches to allow space for a wheelchair to be able to turn. The exact specifications of how an accessible stall should be laid out can be found in the ADA, but the most important thing to think about is, if I were in a wheelchair or using another mobility device, would I be able to comfortably come into the stall with the device and navigate the space?

Improving the Library Experience for Patrons with Mobility Aids

Assess Your Space

Most buildings built today are constructed with accessibility in mind as early as initial planning, which allows for more accessible options. Older buildings tend to be less spacious and can have more issues with creating a fully accessible environment for patrons with any mobility needs.

The first step is to assess the space and see what areas need improvement. Is there a hallway that has too many shelves or chairs making the actual walkway too narrow? Is there enough space between computer desks for a person in a wheelchair to easily move through and turn around? Is the signage at an appropriate height? Some things can't be changed easily, but even taking small measures can make a huge impact on the experience of patrons.

Space is the most crucial aspect of accessibility for those with mobility devices, and crowding can be the biggest barrier to a patron's ability to use the space and can be a major deterrent to patrons wanting to visit.

Communicate with Patrons

Another simple step to take is to develop a plan on how to help patrons who might need assistance either retrieving or finding items. This could be something as simple as making sure to ask every person if they need help finding something or positioning staff members in the stacks ready and able to reach higher or lower items, or to help find items. I know from experience that asking for help with things that are perceived as "simple" can be embarrassing. Sometimes it seems easier to either try to do what I need to do myself or to give up rather than degrade myself. Taking the simple step to ask can make the difference between frustration and defeat and a positive library experience.

It's not advisable to try to determine what a person can or cannot do based on how they look. Asking everyone who walks into the library if they need assistance would help to remove the stigma, but in the event you're speaking with a person using a mobility device and you aren't sure, there are appropriate ways to ask. For example, "Would you feel comfortable following me to the back of the library?" or "Would you feel comfortable reaching down to get this book or would you like me to get it for you?" Phrasing it this way empowers the person to either say they are able to complete the request or need additional help with no judgment.

The most important takeaway is to remember that space is the most crucial aspect of accessibility for those with mobility devices. Crowding can be the biggest barrier to a patron's ability to use the space and even want to visit.

Train Staff

There is an excessive amount of misinformation regarding mobility issues, which can lead to mishaps either in how things are said or done. A good place to start in making the library as accessible as possible after assessing the physical space is to research or develop training on interacting with people who have physical disabilities. Differing bodies or abilities can cause discomfort, which can lead to awkward interactions and situations that could make a patron not feel comfortable returning to the library in the future. Training and open dialogue can help alleviate the discomfort that comes from lack of exposure.

Develop Programming with Mobility Aids in Mind

An extra step that could make a huge difference in the lives of patrons with disabilities is to develop programming with mobility aids in mind. Most programming is planned with the assumption of able-bodied patrons. Not only specifically planning, but also specifically advertising accessible programming can attract patrons who would otherwise assume the activity wouldn't be for them. This can be as simple as ensuring proper space in storytime rooms for any mobility aids or ensuring any outdoor activity either happens on pavement or has an alternate option for patrons unable to navigate grass or dirt.

Small Steps Make a Difference

The world isn't completely accessible yet, but that doesn't mean it won't ever be. It's easy to get comfortable with your own normal; we all do. But what is normal for one person might not be normal for the next, and the safety and comfort of all should be the highest priority of a society. No one is expecting major changes overnight, but every small step makes a difference.

CHAPTER THREE

SPEECH ASSISTIVE TECHNOLOGY

Jackie Kruzie

The word *talk* is widely interpreted as verbal communication, yet at the time of this publication there are approximately four million Americans who are unable to communicate using natural speech.[1] These individuals rely on other forms of communication known as Augmentative and Alternative Communication (AAC). While technology allows nonverbal individuals to talk with assistive devices, there is no assurance they will be heard. This deficit in communication is not due to the lack of ability to engage in conversation, but rather due to the lack of others to listen.

My Story

As a children's librarian, I often visit neighboring libraries to experience other storytime programs and gain ideas to implement in my library. As a mother of a nonverbal child these visits are often filled with anxiety and fear that my daughter will meet rejection, or worse, be ignored. I vividly remember one visit in particular.

> I check the strap attached to my daughter's iPad to ensure it is securely in place before taking her hand and walking into the library. My daughter is excited to go to the "big" library for storytime. We are greeted by a pleasant librarian with an infectious smile and a colorful dress. She bends down to meet my daughter's wondering gaze.
>
> "Hello! What is your name?" she asks.
>
> Silence. The librarian smiles patiently and glances in my direction.
>
> "Tell her your name." I urge and point to the tablet attached to the strap that is draped across her chest.
>
> My daughter quickly enters the code to unlock the tablet. The librarian waves to another child. My daughter taps an icon. The librarian greets another child. A computer-generated voice emanates from the tablet, "My name is Gracie." But the librarian doesn't hear. She has moved on. I smile at my daughter and whisper "Good job." Even though the librarian didn't hear her response, I want her to know that I did. Her words are important, and they deserve to be recognized. ☙

What Everyone Needs to Know

When Gracie was nine months old my husband and I became deeply concerned about her cognitive development. As the parents of four older children, we were well versed in childhood milestones and Gracie had missed too many to ignore. Two years and several evaluations later we were given a diagnosis. Autism. We were advised to seek speech and other forms of therapy to help enhance her skills and aid her development. Over the years some therapies have proved more helpful than others. She has excelled in many areas, yet speech has continued to prove acutely difficult.

When she was seven her speech pathologist recommended aided AAC. So, what exactly is it? AAC modalities are alternative ways a person may communicate.[2] Such ways include, though are not limited to, gestures, sounds, written communication, pictures, photographs, body language, sign language, communication boards, and speech-generating tech devices.

There are various forms of communication. We write, text, and employ the use of emojis and memes. We talk with our hands, gesture, point, roll our eyes, and use other various forms of body language. All of these are examples of unaided AAC. To put it simply, we all use alternate communication to enhance our verbal communication. However, not all of us are capable of verbal communication.

Individuals unable to express their needs verbally rely solely on aided AAC to ensure their message is clear and comprehensive. This means they employ the use of an external device to communicate, such as a tablet, as in my daughter's case. Understanding the difference in unaided and aided AAC is imperative to meeting the communication needs of those who enter your library seeking assistance.

Now that I've given the blanket definitions of unaided and aided AAC, I'll say that I can't share experiences or give examples for all communication modalities. I can only share my experience with speech-generating tech devices as an aided AAC modality. Thanks to modern technological advancements, today's AAC tech assists are often easy to obtain. Electronic handheld devices such as tablets and cell phones can be found at several retail locations or ordered online, and apps for these devices can be purchased and customized to meet the users' specific needs, including a customized voice that is age and gender appropriate for the user. For my daughter, we chose to purchase a small tablet and dedicate it as her "talker," a common term used to describe a personal AAC device. Our daughter's device is a dedicated talker and not used for other activities. For others, their talker may be a cellphone, laptop, or other multi-use device.

There are several communication apps available for purchase through all major mobile app providers. Our daughter uses Proloquo2Go, a symbol-based AAC application. We chose this program because it provides hundreds of symbols and pictures in conjunction with letters and numbers to enrich communication. Gracie is still young and learning how to read and spell. The use of symbols and pictures fit her currents needs while the letters and numbers will be available as her vocabulary and spelling abilities grow. This program also allows us to create complete sentences for common phrases. We created an icon that says, "My name is Gracie," so she could quickly answer this frequently asked question with the touch of a single button. Though her form of communication is different from others, her desire and need to communicate is the same.

What Librarians Need to Know

As librarians we understand the importance of access to information for all and we provide that through various forms of communication. Librarians encounter numerous verbal interactions within a regular work day. Some interactions are small. For example, you may say "thank you" when someone holds open a door allowing you to pass through with your book cart. Other interactions are long. You may spend several minutes probing for more information when a patron asks for the title of that book they remember hearing about with a man and a goat who take a long journey and they think the cover might be orange or maybe yellow, but they can't remember and they are positive you have the title filed away in your mental card catalog. Chances are most of your daily interactions are verbal. You use your voice to fulfill your communication needs. Simply put, communication needs refer to the need to exchange information and as librarians exchanging information is what we do best.

Think back to that small interaction, the one where you said "thank you" to the person holding open the door. Only this time imagine you are the one holding the door. You spot a patron hugging an armload of books struggling to enter the library. You kindly get up and open the door so they can pass through. You smile and say "hello." There is no reply. No "hello." No "thank you." No acknowledgment of any kind. You didn't have to open the door, the least they can do is say thank you, right? But is it really the least they can do? For someone who struggles with verbal communication a simple "hello" or "thank you" may be *more* than they can do.

I am ashamed to admit that at one point I would have been irritated by a person's lack of acknowledgement to my helpful gesture. My attitude changed when my daughter was diagnosed with autism. It was then that I realized verbal communication is a gift. Those who struggle to form words and construct sentences deserve patience, attention, respect, and support. It's important for librarians to extend each of these things to patrons with communication issues.

Many of us may work in libraries where sensitivity and inclusivity training is required. I applaud those who take these trainings seriously. Nothing hurts my heart more than watching my daughter be brushed aside by someone who does not know how to communicate with her. Conversely nothing warms my heart more than seeing her treated with patience and understanding. Yet even with sensitivity and inclusivity training there will remain a level of discomfort when interacting with a patron who cannot speak. When considering the service I wish my child would receive, I came up with a 4-step approach I call The PASS Approach.

The PASS Approach

PASS is shorthand for Patience, Attention, Speak, and Support. Here is a description of these four steps.

Step 1: Patience

When my daughter began using her talker, our speech therapist incorporated her device into every session. At first the focus was to help her learn how to navigate the communication board. Now that she has mastered navigating the program, her sessions focus more on the speed at which she is able to access symbols and form sentences. However, even with practice and daily use, speaking with a talker is not a quick conversation.

Patience is paramount when assisting a patron who uses a speech-generating tech device. While the program is user friendly and simple enough for a young child to navigate, it still takes time to press separate buttons and compose a sentence. Talkers are designed to announce each symbol that is pressed. The user must then press a "go" button before each selected item is read consecutively as a sentence. Simply put, you will hear the sentence twice. Once as they select each symbol, and again when they hit go. For example, How. Are. You. Today. How are you today? Remember to wait for them to hit go before responding.

An AAC program, such as the one my daughter uses, allows only one sentence to be created at a time. Even if the patron has prepared a sentence so they can simply press "go" to have it read aloud, they will still need time to compose another sentence should they require further assistance.

It can take 45 to 60 seconds for my daughter to find the symbol she needs, press it, find the next symbol, press it, find the next symbol, press it, find the next symbol, press it, find the next symbol, press it, find the next symbol, press it, then press go. That was a tedious sentence. Yet to an AAC user they have created a sentence that is concise and to the point at only six words long.

"Where are the dinosaur books please?"

Forty-five seconds may not seem like a long time, but try an experiment. Set a timer for 45 seconds. Now sit and wait for the timer to buzz. Do not continue to read, or check your messages, or sip your drink, just sit and wait.

I'm going to predict it was a lot longer than you anticipated. You may have found it difficult to sit and do nothing for the entire 45 seconds. Now imagine you are the one trying to complete a task while someone waits.

We've all experienced the anxiety that ensues when the grocery store clerk hands you your change and you quickly try to fit the bills into your wallet but there is one errant dollar that refuses to lay flat. The person behind you is inching closer and the clerk is trying to hand you your receipt so you jam the money into the bill slot of your wallet, but you forgot there was change in your hand and you hear the sound of coins hitting the floor. You look down to see two pennies and a dime sprinkled around your feet and you think *it's only 12 cents* so you leave it and hurriedly stuff your bulging wallet—thanks to that one crumpled dollar bill—into your purse as you tell the cashier you don't need the receipt. You grab your groceries and hightail it out of there before the customer behind you starts to get agitated!

The patron using a talker is feeling that same level of anxiety as they compose a sentence. They know you are waiting. Be mindful of their anxiety and assure them that you have time to wait and are happy to assist them in any way.

Step 2: Attention

Take my word for it, you will want to multitask while waiting for the patron to compose a sentence on their device. But don't. Remember that 45-second waiting exercise? I did that to highlight how excruciatingly long you may have to be still while the patron initiates the next part of the conversation. You will want to finish sending that e-mail, continue to unload the book cart, or simply divert your gaze. You will be itching to fill the lag in conversation with an activity. Be aware that doing this will undermine your efforts to put the patron at ease. Your lack of attention will be perceived as impatience, and we already discussed the importance of patience.

My personal tip: observe something about the person you can compliment. That way when they have completed their sentence, you can respond not only to what they have said but also add something to the conversation. "By the way, I like your shoes." Everyone appreciates a compliment, and it will show them that you are fully present.

Giving your full attention may seem like basic advice. After all it's our job to provide all library users with quality service. Yet on average, interactions with patrons are fast paced. You answer a question, direct a patron to their desired book's location, assist with a computer issue, or engage in pleasant easy banter while checking out books, all of which are completed in a matter of moments. An interaction with a patron who uses a talker will take longer than average. Knowing and accepting that from the beginning will help all library staff provide the proper level of attention to ensure the patron is able to access what they need.

Step 3: Speak (Normally)

Requiring the use of a talker does not mean cognitive impairment, hearing impairment, or lack of awareness. The subconscious desire to speak loudly or with a condescending tone is all too real. I cringe when people speak to my daughter in a "baby voice," or worse, when they don't speak to her at all but address me instead. She can't speak, but she is intelligent and aware.

Many people who use a talker will have a caregiver or aide who accompanies them on outings. There are numerous reasons for this, but the use of an aide does not mean the person using the ACC device is incapable of having a one-on-one conversation. When they use their devices to address you, address them back. Be patient, give them your full attention, and keep in mind they will pick up on your tone, your body language, and your capability to address them as an equal. If it's necessary to address the caregiver for clarification, immediately return your attention to the person operating the talker. Don't cut them out of the conversation by addressing only the caregiver. Most important, never speak about the patron to their caregiver as if they're not present.

Step 4: Support

This is the most important step for libraries and librarians. It's imperative that library directors, supervisors, and staff support the use of the PASS Approach. Support must be given not only when interacting with a patron who uses a talker, but also when another staff member is assisting said patron. When you notice a colleague engaged with a talker user, understand that they may be assisting that patron for quite some time. I have been in situations where I was reprimanded for attending to one patron for too long. I was once told that my job is to direct the patron to what they need and move on. This may be acceptable for many patron interactions, but exceptions must be made for patrons with communication issues. Staff and supervisors should support one another and allow ample time to spend with the patron even if that means a daily task is delayed or not completed.

I implemented The PASS Approach when I became the director of a small rural library. A unique opportunity presented itself that allowed me to provide immersive AAC training to the library staff.

One scorching Texas summer day I received a call from my daughter's speech pathologist. She needed to cancel my daughter's therapy appointment due to a broken air conditioner. The unit in her office was broken and would not be fixed for a couple of days. Anyone who has ever set foot in Texas understands that air conditioning is vital. I had a flash of inspiration and quickly suggested she set up shop in the library conference area until the AC unit was functional. Not only would this prevent my daughter's session from being canceled, but it would also benefit all her clients who rely on consistent therapeutic practices to maintain their progress.

The therapist loved the idea and presented it to all her clients. She made sure everyone understood that they could cancel their sessions if they were uncomfortable using a conference room that was visible to the general public. Not a single client canceled. For three days the library saw many new faces enter for therapy and leave with a book. Library staff members were introduced to patrons who used talkers and educated on how to effectively communicate with each of them. The PASS Approach ensured that speech therapy clients who had not visited the library before were met with open arms and encouraged to return. The library was overwhelmed with positive feedback as our new patrons praised us on social media for opening our doors and our hearts to them. It was an incredible experience and showcased the true purpose of libraries—to provide open access to information for all.

What Should Have Happened

Let's rewind and redo the storytime situation from earlier. This incident did not happen at my home library, but at a larger library in a nearby city. Let me be clear that this librarian was kind and welcoming and we enjoyed our time there immensely. Unfortunately, she and the other library staff lacked understanding on how to communicate with an AAC device user. They did not have the PASS Approach knowledge. Had they, this situation could have happened like this:

> We enter the storytime area and a pleasant librarian with an infectious smile and a colorful dress bends down to meet my daughter's wondering gaze.
>
> "Hello! What is your name?" she asks.
>
> Silence. The librarian smiles patiently and glances in my direction.
>
> "Tell her your name," I urge and point to the tablet around her neck.
>
> My daughter quickly enters the code to unlock the tablet. The librarian waves to another child and makes eye contact with a staff member who walks over and begins greeting the arriving children and parents. Gracie taps an icon on her device. The librarian waits patiently. A computer-generated voice emanates from the tablet, "My name is Gracie."
>
> "Hello Gracie, I'm glad you are here today. Please find a seat and we will get started."
>
> Storytime begins on time in an inviting and welcoming atmosphere. ☙

Had the librarian been aware of my daughter's unique communication needs, I have no doubt she would have exhibited patience, given her full attention, spoken to my daughter as she would any other young patron, and would have done so confident that another staff member would take over the duty of welcoming each child as they entered the storytime area.

The PASS Approach (Patience, Attention, Speak, Support) needs to be accepted and incorporated into every library. Directors and management should understand the value of training staff to uphold the principles outlined in the PASS Approach. This inclusive and viable approach is designed to aid librarians in providing quality service and access to information to individuals with communication issues. Whether that information is a request, question, idea, or feeling, the ability to express it verbally is precious and not one everyone shares. As librarians we must be mindful of the limitations that challenge our patrons and incorporate the PASS Approach into our daily interactions.

The responsibility to respectfully meet the communication needs of all those who enter the library is ours. Fulfill it well with knowledge, understanding, and kindness.

NOTES

1. David R. Beukelman and Pat Mirenda, *Augmentative and Alternative Communication: Supporting Children and Adults with Complex Communication Needs*, 4th ed. (Baltimore: Paul H. Brookes Publishing Co., 2013).
2. Jeff Sigafoos, Ralf Schlosser, and Dean Sutherland, "Augmentative and Alternative Communication: Defining and Describing Augmentative and Alternative Communication," in *International Encyclopedia of Rehabilitation* (Buffalo, NY: Center for International Rehabilitation Research Information and Exchange, 2010).

CHAPTER FOUR

BLINDNESS AND LOW VISION

Katherine Schneider

I'm a retired clinical psychologist, blind from birth. As a proud patron of the National Library Service for the Blind for over 60 years and of several university and public libraries over the years, I'd like to give you a snapshot of access to the printed word for blind and visually impaired people. When I was growing up in the 1950s in Kalamazoo, Michigan, the librarian at the Michigan Library for the Blind was my hero. He sent me books in Braille and on records from the Library of Congress through the mail. When those big black boxes of Braille books arrived on the front porch, my anticipation was about as great as it was before Christmas. I knew I would soon be losing myself in a book about somebody else's world.

One of my early Braille favorites was *Brighty of the Grand Canyon.* I can still remember lying and listening to someone reading *Little Women* on records. Then there was the Kalamazoo Public Library which got the first edition of the *World Book Encyclopedia* ever put in Braille, the 1959 edition. To be able to read about any subject under the sun ignited my thirst for knowledge. I wanted to read straight through it, but only got as far as the "C" volumes. I attended a teen book discussion group there, but none of the books were on tape or in Braille, so I just listened. I was able to participate in a way, but not in the way I wanted.

Thankfully, things have changed considerably in the time since I was the kid who sat in a room of people talking about a book I wasn't able to enjoy myself, though there are still barriers yet to be addressed.

An issue for any person looking to get access to accessible professional books and texts is the limited number of accessible texts available. One resource is the Library of Recordings for the Blind (now Learning Ally), a nonprofit organization that provides different learning services to qualifying children including fiction, nonfiction, and textbooks in an audio format. Unfortunately, most books needed for professional attributes are only available in print.

The network libraries of the Library of Congress in each state still provide books on tape and in Braille sent through the mail. The time between publication in print and publication on tape or in Braille has shortened. One might be reading last fall's bestseller in the spring instead of a couple of years later. In addition to receiving books from branches of the Library of Congress, one can also now regularly receive books from Recordings for the Blind and Dyslexic, Xavier Society for the Blind (Catholic lending library), and Bookshare (downloadable versions of books for print-handicapped people). For blind or visually impaired people with computers, the downloadable books are particularly useful for reference books like a first aid book or a recipe book that might be needed months from now when a loaned book from a library would be long gone.

Screen readers are a wonderful addition to today's technology. While there are multiple brands ranging in price from free to around $1,000, each essentially does the same thing: it acts as an interface between the computer or applications—and the person using the device—translating inaccessible text to a more accessible format. While there has been progress towards ensuring accessibility, screen readers don't work on all digital formats or websites yet.

Now with a computer that talks it's simple to go online and scroll through lists of new books at the public library and pick what to be delivered by the Home Delivery Service. Before COVID-19, every three weeks a volunteer brought two bags of CDs, books on tape and print books to my house. We chatted briefly and she left with the bags full of the 21 items she's taking back. I can call a toll-free number and read the last two days of over 200 newspapers through a cooperative venture of the National Federation of the Blind and the National Library Service (NLS) service called Newsline. Or one can use a talking computer to read the portions of my local newspaper posted on its website. In the past, *Newsweek* came on records two months late—now it comes on tape the same week it appears on newsstands. Some movies and television shows have descriptions on a secondary audio programming (SAP) channel, so blind people know who got shot in that mystery they're watching.

It goes deeper than using several libraries and a number of delivery methods to get the information needed to live a full life. It involves librarians who know sources of information and can make recommendations of good books. When I was young, there weren't many books about blind people other than Helen Keller and Louis Braille. To combat this, I started the Schneider Family Book Awards through the American Library Association. They give three awards per year to authors or illustrators of children's books who focused on the disability experience. When children go into the youth area of their libraries now, librarians will be able to recommend books tailored to their situations. Whether they are a child with a learning disability who can read *My Thirteenth Winter* or a blind child with a sighted parent who can read *Looking Out for Sarah* printed both in print and Braille, they'll know that they're not alone.

As our population ages and more people develop visual impairments, libraries, and all providers of books to readers need to consider improving their services to this segment of their customer base. Increasing the number and variety of books in large print and/or on CD, downloading digital talking books for patrons with a NLS player, starting a home delivery service, ensuring that library web pages and online resources are screen reader friendly, and sponsoring readings and book discussions at senior living facilities are a few examples of access possibilities.

What Librarians Should Know

Visual impairment and blindness can happen at any point in life but are more common as people age. Increasingly libraries have stepped up to serving patrons with visual impairments instead of just sending them to the regional library of the National Library Service for the Blind and Print Disabled. This is a good thing because even mid-sized libraries have many more books to offer than the NLS does and can provide reference and programming services too. To be comfortable providing services, library staff may need some training and some resources.

Words and Attitudes

Unfortunately, from primitive times to the present, blindness has been viewed very negatively by those who are uninformed and unaware. Stereotypes of blindness still lurk in the back of our minds. Consider the words that are associated with blindness like "blind fool," "blind rage," and so on. No positives! Stereotypes about blind people include that we are also deaf and/or have cognitive disabilities; that you must talk to the sighted person we're with instead of us; that we're asexual (no need to provide explicit materials or sex education in alternate formats); and that we're amazing and inspirational if we do normal things like going to a discussion at the library.

Although you may be fascinated with how a particular library patron with a visual impairment does daily tasks or how much they can see, stick to questions relevant to their needs, such as "What formats work for you? Large print, Braille, audio?" rather than "How much can you see?" Reading can be done with regular print, large print, audio, or Braille formats and the particular patron you're helping may employ several of these formats. For example, I'm totally blind and if I'm reading a cookbook or a poetry book I might need it in Braille. For a novel, audio or e-book, reading with screen reading technology on my iPhone would be fine.

Tips for Interacting with a Customer Who Is Low Vision or Blind

Greetings

- Say "hi" and tell the person who you are (instead of playing the guessing game, "Hi, do you know who I am?" or just smiling).
- Say "bye" when you leave the room or the conversation. Otherwise, they may be talking to themselves while thinking you're still there.
- If they have a guide dog, ask if you can pet or greet it.
- If there are more than five people around the table at a program, ask each person to say their name so the blind person knows who's sitting where. They can't usually read name tags.

Offering Help

- May I help?
- Let the blind person take your elbow.
- Describe the room and/or tap main pieces of furniture so they know where things are.
- Using nonvisual cues, give directions such as "Go straight ahead of you;" "Go past the machine room on your left;" or "Go to the third carpet."

The most important thing to keep in mind is that this is a library patron. If you make a mistake and say "over there" and point, just apologize and move on to serving them. "Oops, that was silly" is much better than "I'm so so sorry. I shouldn't have said that. . . . " If you say, "Seen any good movies lately?" and then wonder if that was insensitive, notice the patron's reaction. It'll probably just be an answer to your question because we're used to translating *sighted speak.* If you're making an accommodation like reading a PowerPoint slide aloud when giving a talk, don't point out "Because of Kathie, I'll read this"—just do it. Others may benefit and it doesn't feel good to be pointed out in this way. Just pat yourself on the back for skillfully having accommodated a low-vision patron.

Advocating and Becoming an Ally

To meet the needs of blind and low-vision library patrons, library staff may need to advocate with their managers, their boards, their IT departments, their system library, and vendors. A simple request for a book can involve hunting down an accessible version of the book and/or working with Overdrive to make Libby more user-friendly for screen reader users. It's sometimes useful to think of a baseball analogy—for example, getting the book is like hitting a home run and finding the book might be like getting to first base. Just because you ask, doesn't mean the collection development committee will purchase the audio, or that the developers of Libby will be screen reader friendly tomorrow. Getting back to the patron repeatedly with updates is appreciated even when it's not good news that you bear.

Becoming an Ally

Want to go beyond "being nice" and advocating on a particular access issue to becoming an awesome ally for people with visual impairments? Consider some of the following moves:

1. Dig deep; don't take news reports of cures for disabilities or technological fixes for disability issues at face value. Sometimes a press release about a cure being just around the corner means the researchers need more money. Recently Facebook trumpeted that they would label pictures with captions describing them. Labels say things like "may be a person" or "may be outside." That's mildly interesting but it might be good to know if it was the Mona Lisa or Adolf Hitler! Ask people with visual impairments what they think of the new cure or technological fix before getting too excited.
2. Listen to what words you use to describe people with visual impairments. You may show someone a seat, but you don't "put" them there. Our language is full of slights like "I'm so blind!" or "That's really lame." The only way I know to change the sometimes foolish things I say is to listen for them. Maybe some kind soul will tell me but living in the Midwest they may be too polite to do so.
3. Offer help to anyone whether or not they have a visual impairment or other disability if it seems like they need it. Then listen carefully to their response and act accordingly. "Are you okay?" is not an offer; "May I help?" is.

4. Offer to do things with us, not for us. The company is appreciated as much as the help.
5. Get to know us individually. The initial encounter may well be awkward—push on through. If you just know someone with a disability well enough to call them "inspirational," you don't really know them. Just like you, they may be awesome, inspirational, or just plain dull at any given moment.
6. Work to be accessible yourself. Write a few words describing the picture you Tweet or Facebook. Get in the habit of thinking, "If I had a friend who was blind, how would I accommodate them?"

Our "ally radar" will tell us when a great ally is around!

Next Steps

Sometimes a little knowledge is a dangerous thing, but in the case of helping blind and low-vision patrons, it's good. If you know how to sign folks up for the National Library Service for the Blind and Print Disabled, www.loc.gov/nls/; Bookshare, www.bookshare.org; Learning Ally www.learningally.org, and have a contact person at the local low vision support group, the Center for Independent Living, and at your state's Department of Public Instruction, you're well on your way.

Try listening to a described video for 10 minutes with your eyes closed and then open them and watch a bit more with your eyes open. Do the scenes look like you pictured them in your mind when you were just listening? Turn on Voiceover on your iPhone and use one of your favorite apps with your eyes closed to see how accessible it is. Download Blindfold Games and try one (Blindfold Bowling is easy). Then when you're showing something to a patron on their device, you'll have a feel for the steep learning curve and the slowness. You can't glance at the screen to find what you're looking for. You have to listen through all the links when you're listening and not looking.

Best Practices for Library Services to Patrons with Visual Impairments

Listed below are some actionable steps to take and ideas for growth to make sure your library is as accessible as possible for anyone with visual impairments.

Architectural, Interior Design, and Print Considerations

- Use large print name tags for service staff.
- Elevators should include auditory, visual, and tactile signs that are accessible from a seated position.
- Maintain adequate lighting in all areas of the library.
- Use high-contrast signage throughout the library.
- Print publications made available for patrons should use a 12-pt. font that is readable.
- Provide private study rooms for patrons who need to bring personal equipment, require the assistance of a reader, or are distracted by noise and movement.

Staff Considerations

- Have staff trained in assistive computer technology.
- Have staff trained in policies and procedures that provide accommodations to patrons with disabilities.
- Staff should be able to assist patrons with inaccessible electronic resources, either via consultation or by providing those materials in an alternate format.
- Provide reader or research assistants for patrons who are blind or vision impaired.
- Reference and circulation services should be available via phone and e-mail.

- Include a statement on the library's website discussing the library's commitment to accessible materials and activities and inviting patrons with accessibility barriers to speak with staff who will make information resources available.
- Provide home delivery services to take library services to people who have difficulty getting to the library.
- Host storytimes for young children that consider the needs of those with sensory issues; for example, if you're reading a dinosaur book aloud, pass around a model dinosaur.
- Create a purchasing policy that mandates accessibility.
- Board minutes, event publicity, newsletters, and the like should be posted on the library websites.
- Provide an accessible computer station
- Provide access to a Braille printer.
- Provide sign up materials for the National Library Service.
- The library website should meet relevant Section 508 guidelines and Web Content Accessibility Guidelines.
- Provide library videos with audio descriptions where necessary.
- Provide tech training for those learning to use magnification and screen reading options on devices.

Collection Development Considerations

- Include materials in your library's collection on adjusting to low vision.
- Your children's and teens book collections should include books that have won the Schneider Family Book Awards for disability content.
- Choose electronic resources, large print, audio, and print books in the same way all other resources are chosen with topical and popular options available.

- Include movies that have audio description added.
- Your collection should include tactile as well as visual art.
- Include games and puzzles that can be played by blind and low-vision children and youth.

Policy Considerations

- The library's general accessibility policy should include access for people with visual disabilities.
- Maintain a clear complaint procedure for access issues.

Looking for More Tips?

Sheryl Burgstahler, director of DO-IT (Disabilities, Opportunities, Internetworking, and Technology) at the University of Washington, offers a comprehensive list of suggestions for making sure all patrons have equal access to information in both printed and electronic forms in "Equal Access: Universal Design of Libraries." This checklist can be accessed online at www.washington.edu/doit/equal-access-universal-design-libraries.

New Story

With the social distancing of COVID-19 in place as I write this bit, my hopes for a "woke" library experience next time I venture to the library might be a little different. But I would hope that when I enter a staff member would say, "Hi, I'm at the reference desk, may I help you?"

Then I'd ask them how I can get hold of a newspaper story I need for my County Board work. Since the paper's website is not very accessible, the staff member would offer to make a PDF of the article and e-mail it to me. Then I might ask them if there were any good thrillers in audio format on the Lucky Day shelf. If it was indeed my lucky day, they might go above and beyond and recommend a DVD and point out it has audio description. If my newest book, *Hope of the Crow: Tales of Occupying Aging*, had arrived at the library, I might ask if it was displayed in the local authors section or just filed in the social sciences. I'd know that with access to the printed word in alternate formats, if I chose to take part in a book discussion, I wouldn't just sit on the sidelines and listen to others discussing books I couldn't get like I did 50 years ago. Technology has changed a lot to make that possible. With proper training and consideration, I know that I'll have access to the information and entertainment I need to lead a fulfilling life. Then this proud reader and author can go home to dive into another great read.

CHAPTER FIVE

DEAF AND HARD OF HEARING

Cecilia James

I look at the assignment given and know it'll require the help of a librarian. There's no way I could find all the information necessary, and I'd need to use one of their computers with mine still not working. I pull up the website on my phone, scrolling through to find their accessibility options. When I don't find what I'm looking for, I reach out to them via e-mail, asking if they'll be able to accommodate me. It takes a day, but I do get an answer: they can help, but it'll take up to 10 days to be able to do so and they'll only be able to give me 72 hours' notice. I check the due date on the assignment; I'll have enough time but only just. I wonder if it would be worth it to try to find my own interpreter, but that seems more complicated. I reply back that I'll wait to hear back from them and try to do as much as I can in the meantime. ☙

Deafness and the Deaf Community

I am Deaf in one ear and hard of hearing, or HOH, in the other, something I found out at the age of 18 years old when I migrated to the United States. I grew up as a hearing person though I missed hearing many things without recognizing this. Now, at times I feel lost between the deaf community and the hearing community, especially when I cannot hear well, or if my speech is not understood by others as I speak with a lisp. I wish I was exposed to American Sign Language (ASL) at an early age so that it could have been my native language. I definitely can't hear without my hearing aids or even with hearing aids if there is background noise. Approaching a large establishment like a library really makes me timid because though the inside generally has less background noises to make understanding less difficult, I know it has other barriers in the form of lack of specific resources for people who are d/Deaf or HOH, which make it seem less accessible to me.

The d/Deaf and HOH community is composed of people who range on the spectrum of hearing ability. A 2011 study on the prevalence of hearing loss states that:

> We estimate that 30.0 million or 12.7% of Americans 12 years and older had loss from 2001 through 2008, and this estimate increases to 48.1 million or 20.3% when also including individuals with unilateral hearing loss. Overall, the prevalence of hearing loss increases with every age decade.[1]

As is the case with many disabilities, there seems to be a lack of understanding regarding bilateral hearing and how many people are affected by hearing loss in varying degrees. There's also confusion around terminology and the community as a whole. While it would be impossible to explain an entire community in a single chapter, understanding common terms is a good step in the right direction of a better relationship and therefore better inclusion.

Important Vocab

Deaf: lacking the ability to hear sound from birth (generally denoted with a capital D, Deaf).

deaf: lacking the ability to hear either gradually over time or suddenly due to accident, injury, or sickness (generally denoted with a lowercase d, deaf).

Hard of hearing (HOH): diminished hearing either from birth or due to accident, injury, or sickness. Though the ability to hear is less than perfect, there is still some amount of hearing ability left either independently or through the use of devices such as hearing aids.

American Sign Language (ASL): a language expressed through hand motions. ASL is standard in the United States, but forms of sign language exist in other countries as well.

Deaf culture is rich with history, art, and values shared through a common experience. While beautiful and interesting, this culture is often overlooked and misunderstood. Because of its qualities, Deaf culture is considered an ethnic culture by social scientists. While information on the culture can be found in library materials, there are still areas where libraries are lacking to create a fully accessible environment.

On the website of most libraries, you can generally find a service for non-English speaking persons where they can connect directly with a LanguageLine, which is a service that provides both on-site and on-demand translation services in person, via video call, and via phone call. There is a number to connect with an interpreter in various languages. In some cases, this other person may be a library staff member fluent in the language. However, in terms of individuals who are d/Deaf, d/Deaf blind, or HOH, there is no immediate assistance, especially for someone who is Deaf. One must request help and the library may need up to 10 days to fill that request. So, in other words, I can't just walk into a library and expect to be able to speak to someone.. I would need to request an interpreter and possibly wait up to 10 days to actually go and do whatever it was regarding my request for help.

There is a common misconception that just speaking louder will solve all hearing issues, but this belief is wrong on many levels. For those who are d/Deaf, regardless of how loud you speak, the ability to perceive the sound isn't there. For those who are HOH, the level of your voice might not be the issue; it might be how clearly you're speaking, how well you enunciate the words, or how loud the surrounding environment is. Oftentimes, this leads to frustration on both ends. As a person with a lisp, I've often come across issues trying to communicate my needs to librarians. These barriers in communication can cause people to feel like they aren't welcome in a library setting or will require special services that have to be requested prior to entry, making the library seem less accessible.

The Big One: Communication 

The biggest issue facing the d/Deaf community in the general world is communication. While it would be unrealistic to expect everyone to learn sign language, it would have a huge impact to have ASL as a second language be more widely offered. Specifically in a role such as librarian where you're faced with a more diverse range of the population, having ASL—even a beginner's level—as an offered class in an MLS degree program would help tremendously.

Another option that is available is video remote interpreting (VRI). This is a medium where sign language interpreting allows individuals who are deaf or hard of hearing to communicate with a hearing person via videoconferencing. This remote site can host several interpreters who can serve libraries across the county or state. VRI is especially beneficial when (1) there are no available qualified interpreters, and (2) when an interpreter is needed immediately. VRI works by using videoconferencing equipment at multiple locations. The individual who is d/Deaf signs questions to the librarian staff. The interpreter signs everything through a web camera to the person who is d/Deaf. The interpreter is the liaison between the librarian staff and the patron/consumer who is d/Deaf, thus creating a conversation that removes the barriers so everything is understood. By adding something as simple as a teleconference device, a library can ensure they'll always have the ability to communicate with the d/Deaf community .

Three Steps for Communicating with a d/Deaf or HOH person

Certain practices are simple to implement and can have a huge impact on a d/Deaf or HOH person's experience. Here are three simple steps to keep in mind:

1. **Maintain eye contact:** It's easy to get distracted by hand movements or by trying to over-enunciate. It's easier to read ASL and read lips if you as the speaker maintain eye contact.
2. **Be direct:** It's common to use sayings or flowery language to describe and speak. Limit these elaborations in favor of direct instructions.
3. **To get someone's attention,** try physical actions such as
   - touching their shoulder,
   - waving, or
   - turning the lights on and off.

ASL as a Second Language

Many libraries have resources regarding either deaf culture or ASL, and every day more books are written to provide visibility to not only adults, but also children, giving them the chance to feel seen and represented. It's important to not only have these books, but to promote them. This gives everyone the chance to feel represented and to possibly open the doors for hearing people to have a better understanding of their d/Deaf and HOH counterparts.

Libraries that offer English as a Second Language (ESL) programs and classes might want to consider having an ESL class for those whose native language is ASL. While it might seem unneeded, ASL uses entirely different syntax and grammar than English; the discrepancies can lead to issues with reading and writing in English that could be aided by a class offering, or by virtual resources being made available. This could be specifically helpful for children who might not have access to a school for the deaf and therefore lack the resources to develop language the way it would be taught in a traditional school.

Another thing to keep in mind is attempting to make each program as accessible as possible. That could mean doing something as simple as ensuring captions are on for any video program or implementing an ASL storytime for a children's program.

Accessibility in Action 

The key to having a truly accessible library is opening the doors for good communication with the d/Deaf and HOH community, which can present more challenges than the hearing population, but that doesn't make it less important. Setting up training for library staff to learn and implement small steps for getting attention would be a good first step. While it might not be possible to set up video remote interpreting at every library, making an effort to ensure that at least one library in a given county has access to an interpreter would go a long way. Putting an emphasis on hiring people who can sign or providing the resources and motivation to current staff to learn how to sign would also be great strides towards making the library a safe and comfortable place for everyone.

Looking Ahead

I look forward to the day when I can walk into a library and know that my preferred method of communication will be understood, when I don't have to plan a simple trip 10 days in advance. I can't wait for the day that I can walk into a library and use all the resources provided just like any other patron.

NOTE

1. Frank R. Lin, John K. Niparko, Luigi Ferrucci, "Hearing Loss Prevalence in the United States," *Archives of Internal Medicine* 171, no. 20 (2011): 1851–1853, doi:10.1001/archinternmed.2011.506.

CHAPTER SIX

LEARNING DIFFERENCES

Alex Kerr

It all started with a spark. I was in second grade, struggling in class, and in my seat in the back I decided to try something. I had seen a documentary on the discovery of electricity and how in France they would run low electrical current through metal rods so people could feel the electricity. Curious about this experience with a low current, I inserted a pair of scissors in the electrical outlet, making sure to hold on to the rubber handle since rubber does not conduct electricity. As the rest of the class turned in horror, the sparks flowed over my small wooden desk. I sat unharmed but in trouble. The main result was my mother—who worked at the school—decided to have me take a series of tests designed to evaluate academic abilities. She wanted to know how a bright child who loved history and literature could be struggling so much in class. The test confirmed I had learning disabilities. ☙

Learning Differences Explained

The Learning Disabilities Association of America website states, "Learning disabilities are due to genetic and/or neurobiological factors that alter brain functioning in a manner which affects one or more cognitive processes related to learning. These processing problems can interfere with learning basic skills such as reading, writing and/or math. They can also interfere with higher level skills such as organization, time planning, abstract reasoning, long or short-term memory and attention. It's important to realize that learning disabilities can affect an individual's life beyond academics and can impact relationships with family, friends and in the workplace."[1]

I was lucky on two accounts: I wasn't electrocuted, and secondly, that my mother, a special needs educator, knew the signs of learning disabilities. She was already aware of the genetic component of learning disabilities, and knowing that both my father and brother have learning disabilities, she was better prepared to notice the signs in me. Working at the school also allowed her to know my teachers and pay close attention to my academic struggles.

Learning disabilities, in my own words as someone who has lived with them, are like putting together a piece of Ikea furniture without the instructions or tools. Most people see the instructions and can match the pieces, parts, and tools to build a piece of furniture. For me, I could understand that something needed to happen to make it look like the end product, but no matter how I tried I could not follow the instructions, so I needed to create directions that worked for me.

What Are Learning Disabilities?

Learning disabilities (LD) are often described as a hidden disability. Often LD students suffer academically before being tested. Their teachers might describe them as bright but just a little slow. Their difficulties can take many shapes. Some people with learning disabilities have trouble spelling and writing, sometimes reversing letters and words. Others have trouble reading in general without losing their place or reading out loud or at a steady pace. Others struggle to recall information. This ranges from trying to remember a specific word or recall a conversation.

These difficulties can be frustrating and can leave those with LD feeling disheartened; they may tune out the lessons or do just enough to get by. This is the drawback of learning disabilities; people that could be exceptional are dismissed as being slow. We hear it on a TV show, movie, or maybe in our lives when someone says quietly, "he/she is just a little slow." The truth could be that they just learn in a different way and need some tools to help them bridge the gap to understanding and knowledge. These tools may seem simple, and may seem natural to some, but for someone with learning disabilities they can be life changers.

Understanding Learning Styles

Most people, even people without learning disabilities, have a way that's easier for them to learn and absorb new information. Some people learn easiest by listening while others learn best by observing. Others are kinesthetic learners, which means they retain information better by doing. Knowing an individual's learning style is especially important for individuals with learning disabilities because it allows them to develop and use techniques to assist in the retention of information that may otherwise be difficult to learn.

Tools for LD Learners

Bookmarks are a powerful tool for people with LD. Take that trusty bookmark, turn it sideways and you can use it to cover the lines below the one you are reading. This allows the eyes to focus on just the line currently being read and not get overwhelmed by the block of words below it. It might seem simple, but to a child who is a slow reader and struggles with reading, it can help them take a book line by line and realize that, on their own, they actually read the whole thing.

Blocks of text are not the only thing that distracts and bogs down LD readers. An unknown word can stop a reader in their tracks. The often-taught technique of sounding out the parts of the word doesn't work for everyone. It's too easy to fixate on the word and get discouraged. To combat this, encourage readers to skip words they don't know. Skipping words allows readers to keep going without feeling defeated.

Another tool to assist with reading is to read along with an audiobook. This tool is pretty popular now with digital services provided for adults and children alike. Libraries provide TumbleBooks, which feature talking books for kids, and Amazon has a function called WhisperSync for their e-books that allows a reader to listen to the audiobook while words highlight in tandem in the e-book.

For some people, LD includes becoming overwhelmed by information, and consequently being unable to focus. This inability to focus makes it challenging to work or to achieve anything and can leave people with LD feeling defeated. To work around the predicament, encourage students and patrons to stop and refocus when overwhelmed by information. Help them to break down information, to see what is being said, and what is being asked. Consider making a list of the information. Once the information is broken down, it is much easier to see what's needed. This technique can help to reduce information overload. The technique also encourages empathy. It helps people to focus and stay on track.

Bad spelling skills are a common sign of learning disabilities. Encourage students and patrons to replace words they cannot spell with ones they can that have the same meaning. Share the spell check tool in Microsoft Word along with its thesaurus function. Enable the Microsoft Word read aloud to function to read back what was written. This allows students and patrons to listen for sentence flow and spelling.

Another tool is to draw out or talk out ideas or words. There may be times when someone with LD may know what's in their head but are unable to express it. This can get very frustrating, so to help, talk around the idea or draw out the idea visually. This will encourage getting the idea or words out instead of being stuck and unable to communicate.

Sharing the Wonder of Books

You might not think those with learning disabilities would become readers or enjoy books, but you'd be mistaken. To grow LD readers, start by offering them stories that interest them and use those subjects and stories to build on to expand their reading. If your student/patron likes baseball, try a book on the history of the game, or a player's biography, or a work of fiction with a baseball element. If they're really lost, ask what movies they like. They can usually answer that question, which provides a foundation to build on.

Training Staff

There are many techniques you can use when training staff. First, start with a focus on patience and enjoyment. Display a relaxed attitude that allows mistakes to happen with the understanding that mistakes are learning experiences. Keeping staff relaxed helps them absorb the information.

Here are some additional tips for accommodating the different styles of learning: seeing (visual learners), by hearing (auditory learners), by taking notes (reading/writing learners), or by doing (kinesthetic learners) and creating an inclusive training experience.

- Go over the training packet and schedule, so everyone knows what to expect and won't get overwhelmed or nervous.
- Ask attendees if they have a learning style they favor, which usually means asking if they're a notetaker and hands-on learner. Most people aren't aware of the different learning styles but asking if they are a notetaker (reading/writing) or a hands-on (kinesthetic) learner can help you understand their learning needs.
- When training, offer a notepad in case staff want to take notes and ask if they need any information to be repeated or if they need the information presented more slowly. Always repeat information and go slower so that they can jot down information and be active in the training process.
- Provide a set of written instructions/quick guides of tasks they're required to learn, along with a vocabulary bookmark for terms that they might be unfamiliar with, and other fun information. The written instructions/quick guides engage the reading/writing learners who need to read and take notes for their learning foundation. Explain what the quick guides are and that the instructions are theirs to keep and do what they want with them. They can write on them and highlight certain steps—whatever they need to do to help them with learning the task.
- Next, model the tasks as you explain the different ways to do things, the reason why some ways are done, and the expected final step which must happen. This observation portion of the training is for the visual learners who will see you acting out the different ways and the verbal explanations are for the auditory learners who need

to hear to learn. Incorporate visual and auditory learning styles during the observation training.

- When possible, show multiple people doing the same task so that trainees can see that there are multiple ways to reach the final step and one way is not better than another. It also helps to incorporate the handouts/quick guides during this training phase. Refer to the handout/quick guide, reading the steps and performing them as you go to strengthen the learning experience by incorporating three learning styles at once.
- Once the trainee has completed the observation portion of the training, incorporate the kinesthetic learning style by asking the trainee to do the task as you guide them. During this time pay attention to the trainee, observing if they need more or less guidance, and answer any questions. Allow for mistakes and softly correct if necessary. Again, refer to the handout/quick guide to read aloud as they do the task again to incorporate three learning styles at once with them doing, reading the instructions, and hearing the instructions as they are read.
- Lastly, create verbal quizzes and explain that you are looking to see if they understand or need to review. In the quizzes, ask how to do something and allow staff to answer by talking it out or acting it out.

Training in this way will allow you to connect to each of the major learning styles.

Learning Is the Spark

If I didn't have learning disabilities, I wouldn't have the knowledge of different learning styles. The LD classes that I took as a child taught me the different learning styles so I could find what style worked best for me to learn. This encouraged me to search inward to understand the way my brain works so I can succeed. It helped me find a style of learning that works for me and gave me several tools I use. Most students are not given this information or opportunity. They are able to process information without needing to really think about how they are doing it. The ability to learn so easily may be good, but by not stopping and exploring the way they learn, many people may miss out on other ways to learn that may work better for them.

Library staff can share information using the four different learning styles whether they are interacting with someone with a learning disability or not. This inclusive way of teaching will allow for better communication and understanding by showing that everybody learns about the world differently and therefore experiences the world differently.

Learning can and should start with a spark, but maybe not a literal spark. There are hundreds of interventions for people with learning disabilities, and more being developed daily, that can help to make sure that we can all thrive in modern society. The spark this needs to start with is by not only learning the easy things to spot in children and adults that can indicate learning disabilities, but also to become familiar with the tools and resources available so they can be used by all, and what better place to foster that kind of innovation than a library?

NOTE

1. Learning Disabilities Association of America, "Types of Learning Disabilities," https://ldaamerica.org/types-of%20learning-disabilities/.

CONCLUSION
Communication Is Key

Kodi Laskin

It's normal to fear the social repercussions of asking questions that might be perceived as too personal or inappropriate. Unfortunately, this fear can lead to misunderstandings and an inadequacy of services available to people with different needs. When I realized the unique position I was in as both a frontline library employee and a person with a disability, I decided to use that knowledge to bridge the gap between the two groups. Libraries have been a safe place for me, a place of refuge and acceptance. I've always been fortunate to have good experiences in libraries, and I firmly believe that everyone, regardless of what they're using the library for, should be able to find what they're looking for within those walls. My hope is that this book will provide a good jumping off point to open up the conversation and make the goal of accessibility more attainable.

No one is expecting everything to be fixed overnight; many barriers to accessibility are long-term considerations, but even small steps, something as simple as being more patient with a child using a speech generating device, or taking a couple sign language classes, could mean the difference between a patron feeling they shouldn't come back and feeling both accepted and welcome. The more these lines of communication stay open with both sides trying to understand the other, the better the chances of a truly accessible world.

ABOUT THE CONTRIBUTORS

CECILIA JAMES is the founder and executive director of I Hear You, Inc. and author of *From Inside the Shell.* She also works with the Starkey Hearing Foundation to give the gift of hearing to those who need it and with the Internal Revenue Service to create programs for individuals who are d/Deaf and hard of hearing.

LEAH KEEVAN is an enthusiast of sewing, prop making, costuming, and writing. She has used her writing and her voice to advocate for disability rights and works to make the world a more accessible place.

ALEX KERR is a Florida native. He graduated from Florida Atlantic University with a bachelor's degree in English. He currently works at the Boca Raton Public Library as a team lead in the Account Services section.

JACKIE KRUZIE has a Master of Library Science. She worked in both public and school libraries before transitioning into publishing. She is a picture book author and acquisitions editor at Blue Whale Press, an imprint of Clear Fork Publishing, focusing on STEM books for children. Her website, jackiekruzie.com, features storytime picks for librarians and teachers.

KATHERINE SCHNEIDER is a retired clinical psychologist living in Eau Claire, Wisconsin, with her tenth seeing eye dog. Schneider has published a memoir, a children's book, two books for seniors, and originated the Schneider Family Book Awards for children's books with disability content. Subscribe to her blog at https://kathiecomments.wordpress.com for details.

INDEX

V

W